CHAIN REACTIONS

# From Cowpox to Antibiotics

## Discovering Vaccines and Medicines

Dr. Carol Ballard

Heinemann Library
Chicago, Illinois

Consultant: Professor Christopher Lawrence
Commissioning editor: Andrew Farrow
Editors: Kelly Davis and Richard Woodham
Proofreader: Catherine Clarke
Design: Tim Mayer
Picture research: Amy Sparks
Artwork: William Donohoe p. 15

Originated by RMW
Printed and bound in China
by Leo Paper Group

11 10 09 08
10 9 8 7 6 5 4 3 2 1

Library of Congress Cataloging-in-Publication Data
Ballard, Carol.
    From cowpox to antibiotics : discovering vaccines and
medicines / Carol Ballard.
        p. cm. --  (Chain reactions)
    Includes bibliographical references and index.
    ISBN 978-1-4034-8839-8 (hc)
    ISBN 978-1-4329-0697-9 (sc)
    1. Vaccines--History--Juvenile literature. 2.
Vaccination--History--Juvenile literature. 3.   Antibiotocs-
-History--Juvenile literature. 4. Chemotherapy--History--
Juvenile literature.  I. Title. II. Series.
    QR189.B35 2007
    615'.372--dc22

                    2006010001

Acknowledgments
The author and publishers are grateful to the following
for permission to reproduce copyright material:
Corbis pp. 8 (Bettmann), 10 (CDC/PHIL), 12 (Burstein
Collection), 13 (Bettmann), 27 (Bettmann), 32–33
(Bettmann), 50 (Dennis Degnan); Exile Images pp. 25
(H. Ruiz)/USCR), 43 (H. Davies); Popperfoto p. 44; Science
Photo Library pp. 1 (Russell Kightley), 4 (Mark Clarke),
5 (Mark Thomas), 6 (Robert Brook), 16, 18–19 (Dr. Gopal
Murti), 23, 26 (TH Foto-Werbung), 29 (Colin Cuthbert),
30 (National Library of Medicine), 31 (St. Mary's
Hospital Medical School), 34, 35 (Andrew Lambert
Photography), 36 (Kwangshin Kim), 39 (K.R. Porter),
41 (CDC), 45 (Tek Image), 46 (Hank Morgan), 47
(Maximilian Stock Ltd), 52 (Alexis Rosenfeld), 54
(Russell Kightley), 55 (Geoff Tompkinson), cover
(Tek Image); Topfoto.co.uk pp. 7 (ARPL), 9 (HIP/Ann
Ronan Picture Library), 11 (Oxford Science Archive),
14 (Ann Ronan Picture Library/Albert Edelfelt), 21
(La Nature 1886), 24, 37 (Boyer/Roger-Viollet), 38
(Boyer/Roger-Viollet), 48 (Zoriah/The Image Works),
49 (Public Record Office/HIP).

Cover design by Tim Mayer.

Every effort has been made to contact copyright holders
of any material reproduced in this book. Any omissions
will be rectified in subsequent printings if notice is given
to the publisher.

The paper used to print this book comes from
sustainable resources.

# Contents

Any words appearing in the text in bold, **like this**, are explained in the Glossary.

# From Putting on Bandages to Saving Lives

Can you remember the last time you fell over and cut your knee? It probably hurt, and may have been uncomfortable for a few days afterward. But you would not have expected it to have been any more serious than that, would you? Yet there was a time when injuries that we now regard as minor were serious and even life-threatening!

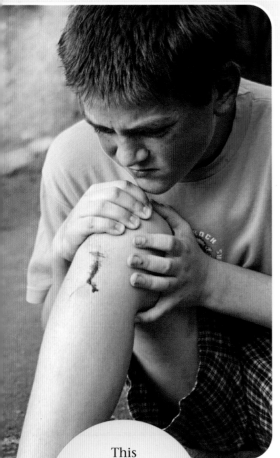

This 11-year-old boy has cut his knee. But, as long as he keeps the cut clean, it is very unlikely to get infected.

Going back to that cut knee... Can you remember what you did about it? You probably mopped up the blood and washed the cut with clean water. You might have used an **antiseptic** wipe, cream, or spray. You might have covered the cut with a bandage. But what did people do in the days before the discovery of antiseptics? And before anybody knew why you should clean the wound? How have people found out that these things are important? How have our everyday lives changed so that we can deal quickly and easily with injuries such as this?

You have probably heard about children being **vaccinated** against a range of diseases, or about people needing vaccinations before they travel to distant countries. You might even have had some of these injections yourself. Vaccinations provide protection against some very nasty diseases that can cause severe illness or even death. But what did people do before vaccines existed? And what made somebody think that it might be possible to protect people in this way? How did they try out their ideas? What happened in their early experiments?

This book will tell you about the chain of scientific ideas, experiments, and discoveries that led to the very first vaccine. It will also explain the development of some medicines that we take for granted today. Some discoveries are the result of a single person's research and ideas. Many breakthroughs, though, come from a whole team of scientists working together. Few discoveries arise from nowhere. Most are built on the steps other scientists have already taken. These discoveries, in turn, become the steps for the next scientists to build on.

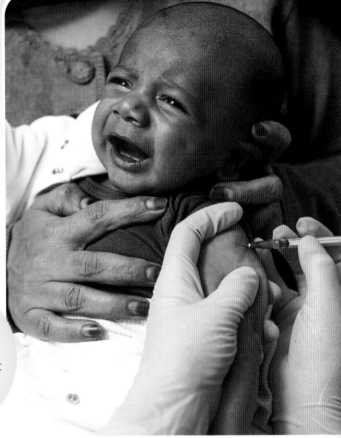

This four-week-old baby boy is being vaccinated against **tuberculosis (TB)**.

## HOW DO MEDICINES WORK?

We use medicines to help us stay fit and healthy. They can work in one of three ways:

1. They can prevent an illness from beginning. For example, vaccines can stop us from catching certain diseases, such as measles.
2. They can cure an illness. For example, **antibiotics** can get rid of infections, such as **tonsillitis**.
3. They can relieve illness, even though we are still sick. For example, painkillers can make things hurt less.

# Before Modern Medicines

People in the past tried to heal their illnesses and injuries by using plants and other things that they found in the world around them. If something worked, they would use it again and pass the information on to others. In this way different medical traditions slowly developed. Some ideas from the worlds of ancient Egypt, China, Greece, and India were written down and have survived.

## THAT'S AMAZING!

Some ancient Egyptian remedies worked well, such as putting moldy bread on cuts to help them heal. But other remedies, such as eating mud and animal dung, probably made the patients feel worse!

These carvings on an Egyptian temple show a range of medical instruments, including hooks, bone saws, measuring spoons, scales, lances, chisels, and dentistry tools.

## Medicine in ancient times

More than 4,000 years ago, Egyptian doctors were famous for their skill. Imhotep, for instance, was a respected doctor, who was made the god of medicine after his death. Ancient Egyptians believed that each part of the body was looked after by a different god. But the doctors made their own decisions about how to treat illnesses. They had a range of medicines, and each medicine was used for a particular illness.

In ancient China, people believed that the body was controlled by two forces: yin and yang. When these two forces were balanced, the person was healthy. When the two forces were not balanced, the person got sick. All the medical treatments were therefore intended to rebalance the yin and yang. Some of the remedies used in ancient China were recorded in a book called the *Pen T'sao*. Chinese traditions say this information was collected by Shen Neng over 5,000 years ago.

Meanwhile in ancient India a system of natural medicine called Ayurveda took over from magic and religious beliefs. Ayurveda was based on the use of plants as medicines, and it is still widely practiced in modern India.

In ancient Greece most people believed in many gods. They thought some of these gods controlled health and disease. Asclepius was the god of medicine.

### HIPPOCRATES' STORY

Hippocrates of Cos was a Greek doctor and teacher around 400 B.C. He taught that doctors should observe and examine patients carefully. By doing this, a doctor could find out what was wrong and **prescribe** a suitable remedy. This was a new way of thinking. It marked an important step forward in learning how to treat patients. Hippocrates also set out rules that said doctors should always act for the good of the patient. These rules form part of a doctors' promise, which is called the Hippocratic Oath. Hippocrates is often described as "The Father of Medicine."

This is a bust of the Greek physician Hippocrates of Cos.

7

## The Middle Ages and beyond

In Europe much of the knowledge from the ancient civilizations was gradually lost, but some ideas were passed on. In the Middle Ages (A.D. 1100–1500), the Christian Church was powerful and important in most of Europe. Medicine therefore had to fit in with the Church's teachings.

During this period many people turned to monks for healing and medicines. Others relied on local "wise women." Both monks and wise women used many plant remedies. Books in which these remedies were written down were called herbals.

Most medicine at the time was based on the work of Galen (A.D. 129–c. 216), a Greek doctor who worked in Rome for many years. He taught his students to take a patient's **pulse** and look at his or her urine to **diagnose** diseases. He believed that accurate diagnosis was vital. He also insisted that doctors study the human body to understand how it worked.

### THAT'S AMAZING!

In the Middle Ages, doctors often thought patients needed to lose blood. Sometimes they put blood-sucking worms, called leeches, on the patient's skin to suck blood out. In other cases, they cut one of their patient's veins to let some blood drain away. Treatments such as this only made the patient weaker!

This illustration from the 1100s shows a medieval herbalist supervising the gathering of medicinal plants.

Another important person was Avicenna (also known as Ibn Sina), an Arab doctor. He studied Galen's work and based his own writings and teachings on it. Avicenna's books were an important source of written information for doctors and medical students for many years.

By the early 1500s, people were beginning to question many of the Church's teachings about science and medicine. The Church's authority was being challenged. At the same time, new medical ideas arose.

## PARACELSUS' STORY

The person known as Paracelsus (1493–1541) was born in Switzerland. His real name was Philippus Aureolus Theophrastus Bombastus von Hohenheim, but he changed it when he left school. He was a scientist and doctor, but he disagreed with many of Galen's and Avicenna's ideas. Paracelsus changed the way doctors thought. For instance doctors had previously made medicines using plant and animal matter. Paracelsus tried using minerals, such as copper, iron, and lead, to treat diseases. He also used mercury, a liquid metal, to treat an infectious disease called syphilis. This was the first time a mineral had been shown to work as a medicine. However, mercury is actually a poison, so his patients suffered unpleasant side effects.

The Swiss-born doctor Paracelsus recognized the importance of chemistry in medicine.

# The First Vaccine

For medicine to progress, doctors needed to find out more about diseases. Some of the most common diseases are infectious. This means that they can pass from one person to another. Infectious diseases can spread quickly within a family, and through a village, town, or city. At the end of the 1700s, the only way to prevent diseases from spreading was to isolate anyone who became infected. The idea was that if no one went near the infected person, the disease could not spread. However, by the time a person was obviously ill, it was too late. The infected person had probably already passed the disease on! People desperately needed some form of protection against this type of disease.

**Smallpox** was particularly dangerous. Many people who caught it, especially children, died. Those who did not die were left very badly scarred. In the 1600s, more than 60 million Europeans died of smallpox. Settlers from Europe carried smallpox to the United States. The native peoples had no **resistance** to this new disease, and therefore many died of it.

A patient in Ghana, photographed in 1967, shows scabs caused by smallpox. The scabs eventually fall off, leaving pitted scars.

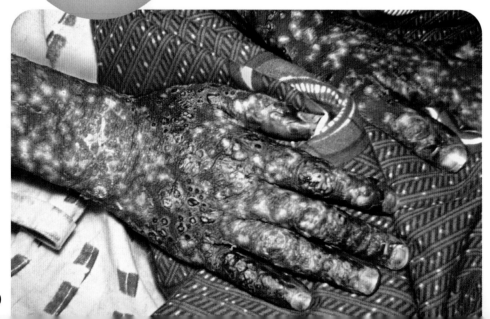

10

## Edward Jenner and cowpox

In 1796 an English country doctor named Edward Jenner (1749–1823) made a very important breakthrough. His discovery was the first step toward finding a way to control some infectious diseases. He found a way of **vaccinating** people against smallpox.

People who lived near Jenner believed a country tale about cowpox and smallpox. They thought that cowpox (a disease similar to smallpox, but much milder) would protect them against smallpox. Dairymaids, who often caught cowpox from the cows they worked with, rarely caught smallpox. Jenner thought this was interesting and decided to investigate. Would it be possible to infect people with cowpox on purpose, and could this protect them from smallpox? This seemed a strange idea, but perhaps it would work.

This portrait of Edward Jenner was painted by Charles Knight in 1837.

## ? HOW DID INOCULATION WORK?

Before the late 1700s, **inoculation** was the only protection against smallpox. Inoculation had been used in China, India, and other places since ancient times. **Pus** was taken from the spots of someone with smallpox, and injected into a healthy person. This usually caused a mild case of smallpox, and the person soon recovered. The person would then be resistant to smallpox infection in the future. However, not all cases were mild, and many healthy people died from smallpox caused by inoculation. It also spread smallpox to other people.

## Smallpox protection?

In May 1796 there was an outbreak of cowpox at a local farm. Jenner met a girl called Sarah Nelmes, who had cowpox. He decided to carry out an experiment. First, he took some pus from Sarah. Then he made some scratches on the arm of a healthy boy, James Phipps. Jenner spread the pus from Sarah over the scratches and waited to see what would happen. As he expected, James became ill with cowpox. This proved that the first part of Jenner's idea would work. He could purposely infect people with cowpox.

The next stage of Jenner's work was crucial. Would his method actually succeed in providing protection against smallpox?

About six weeks later, Jenner did the next part of his experiment. Again, he made scratches on James Phipps' arm and spread pus over the scratches. This time, though, the pus was from a smallpox patient. Jenner waited to see whether James Phipps would actually get smallpox or whether the cowpox would protect him.

## THAT'S AMAZING!

One of the first people to be vaccinated against smallpox in the United States was President Thomas Jefferson (1743–1826). Jefferson was president from 1801 to 1809. Before entering politics, he was trained as a lawyer. He was a highly educated man who was very interested in science, the arts, and education. This portrait was painted by Gilbert Stuart in about 1805.

Luckily for James he did not get smallpox. Jenner's idea had worked. At last there was a way to protect people against smallpox!

Jenner repeated his technique on more people, including his own baby son. He was successful every time. However, he found it hard to persuade doctors and scientists that his method worked. Other doctors tried to repeat his methods, but some of their patients died as a result of the doctors' carelessness and mistakes. Gradually, though, his ideas became widely accepted and his method became popular.

## Storing and transporting vaccine

The next step was for Jenner to find a way of storing the pus, so that he could treat people when fresh cowpox pus was not available. Jenner discovered that pus could be dried and stored for three months and still be effective. The dried pus could be sent abroad. This meant that other doctors, in other countries, would be able to use the treatment.

Jenner's technique became known as vaccination, and the injected material as vaccine. This name was from the scientific name for cowpox, which was vaccinia. Jenner's work has saved the lives of millions of people who, without vaccination, would have died from smallpox. It also paved the way for the development of vaccines against other infectious diseases.

Ali Maow Maalin, of Merka, Somalia, had the world's last recorded case of smallpox in 1977. Thanks to a World Health Organization vaccination campaign, there have been no recorded cases of smallpox since then.

# The Importance of Microbes

Although Jenner's vaccination method could prevent people from catching **smallpox**, nobody knew what actually caused infectious diseases. The work of two scientists, Louis Pasteur (1822–1895) and Robert Koch (1843–1910), eventually solved the puzzle.

Louis Pasteur was a French scientist, who was very interested in chemistry. He began to investigate the process of making wine from grapes. At the time, people knew that wine contained **microbes** called yeast.

This painting shows Louis Pasteur, the French chemist and biologist, in his laboratory.

## Microbes in the air

If Pasteur covered the grapes with fine cloth, they did not **ferment** and produce alcohol. The cloth seemed to stop the yeast microbes from getting to the grapes. He thought this must be because there were yeast microbes in the air. He carried out some experiments to test this idea.

Pasteur collected air from places at different altitudes (heights). When he exposed grape juice to air from high altitudes, there was less fermentation than with air from lower altitudes. This made him think that the higher air was cleaner than the lower air. The higher air seemed to contain fewer microbes.

Pasteur's next experiment proved his idea beyond doubt. He put some liquid into a **sterile** glass flask. He then heated the neck of the flask and pulled it out into a swan's neck shape. He sealed the end of the neck so that nothing could get in or out. The liquid did not ferment.

Then Pasteur broke the end of the neck. Now air could get in, but dust and microbes would be trapped on the inside of the glass neck. There was no fermentation. But when he tipped the flask, some of the liquid touched the inside of the neck. After this, the liquid began to ferment. The fermentation could only have been caused by microbes that had entered the flask on dust in the air. Pasteur had proved that there are microbes in the air.

This diagram shows how Pasteur carried out his swan's neck flask experiment in order to test whether dust in the air could **contaminate** a liquid.

sealed neck

neck broken, allowing dust and microbes to enter

microbes multiply, causing liquid to ferment

sterile liquid

## HOW CAN MICROBES BE KILLED?

Pasteur also did some work that proved that heat could kill the microbes that turned wine and beer sour. This was the beginning of the heat-treatment process we now call **pasteurization**. For example, we use pasteurization to treat milk and other products to keep them from going bad. Pasteur also realized that heat might help to prevent the spread of infectious diseases, but it needed other scientists to develop this idea further (see pages 22–25).

This illustration is in a book from the 1800s. It shows microbes as seen under a microscope.

## Do microbes cause disease?

After Pasteur's discovery that there were microbes in the air, scientists began to wonder whether these microbes might cause infectious diseases. But studying microbes was difficult. Robert Koch, a German doctor and scientist, solved this problem by developing a way of growing microbes in the laboratory.

**Anthrax** was an infectious disease that killed sheep and cattle. A French scientist, Casimir Joseph Davaine (1812–1882), showed that there were microbes in the blood of diseased sheep. He also found that there were no microbes in the blood of healthy sheep. When healthy sheep were injected with blood from the diseased sheep, they too became ill. The same microbes then also appeared in the blood of the sheep he had injected. Davaine thought this showed that there must be a link between the microbes in the blood and the anthrax disease.

## Finding out more about microbes

Robert Koch decided to investigate further. He took microbes from the blood of infected animals and studied them under his microscope. He was then able to describe all the stages in the life cycle of a microbe. This was the first time that anyone had studied how a microbe develops.

Robert Koch wanted to continue studying microbes. In order to do so, he needed to be able to grow microbes in his laboratory. From the work of another scientist, Joseph Schroeter, Koch knew that colonies of microbes would grow on foods, such as bread and potatoes. Koch used this knowledge to work out a recipe for a mixture of nutrients in which microbes would grow. He could use this mixture, called a **culture**, to grow microbes in the laboratory. He also found a way of making sure that the colonies of microbes stayed pure and did not become contaminated by other types of microbe.

Koch went on to study infected wounds. He isolated six different microbes in the wounds and grew pure cultures of them. He injected these into healthy animals and then isolated the same microbes from the injected animals.

## WHAT ARE KOCH'S RULES?

Based on his work on microbes from infected wounds, Koch worked out a set of rules for infectious diseases:

● a specific microbe is always associated with the disease

● the microbe can be isolated from an infected animal and grown in pure culture

● the microbe that has been grown will cause the same disease if it is injected into a healthy animal

● the same type of microbe can be isolated from the injected animal.

Koch said that these rules would always be true if a specific microbe caused a specific disease.

## Germs

By the end of the 1870s, Robert Koch had shown that there was a link between microbes and infectious diseases. However, many scientists still did not completely believe him. Could there be something else in the culture that caused disease? Louis Pasteur was determined to prove that microbes were indeed the cause of infectious diseases. From all this work came one of the most important ideas about disease: the Germ Theory.

Louis Pasteur took Robert Koch's work a step further. He took one drop of blood from an anthrax-infected animal and put it into 50 milliliters of culture. He left the mixture for a long time to let the microbes grow. Then he took one drop of the culture and added that to 50 milliliters of fresh culture liquid. Again, he left the mixture to let the microbes grow. He repeated this process 100 times.

These cholera bacteria are seen under a powerful microscope.

The final solution contained hardly any of the original culture liquid. But it did contain microbes because they had been allowed to grow at each stage. When Pasteur injected the final mixture into a healthy animal, it became infected with anthrax. The only thing that could have caused this was the microbes. This experiment proved beyond any doubt that microbes could cause an infectious disease.

### Protecting chickens against cholera

Louis Pasteur then began to study chicken cholera, a disease that killed chickens rapidly and was a real problem for farmers. He isolated the microbe that caused the disease and stored it in his laboratory. Later he was amazed to find that his fresh cultures of microbes transferred the infection. His stored cultures, though, did not. If he then injected fresh culture into chickens that had previously had stored culture, they did not become ill! It looked as if his stored culture was protecting the chickens against cholera.

Pasteur realized that this was similar to Edward Jenner's work with cowpox. But this time the microbes that gave protection did not cause any disease themselves because they were weak or dead. Might this work with other infectious diseases?

## WHAT IS THE GERM THEORY?

The Germ Theory, developed during the 1870s, says: "Microbes cause infectious diseases." This theory was the result of several scientists working in different countries. The link between microbes and infectious diseases had finally been proved. Knowing what caused infectious diseases was an important step in finding ways of preventing and curing these diseases. For example, once people knew that coughing and sneezing could pass on the microbes that cause the common cold, they realized that using a handkerchief could help to prevent the illness from spreading.

## Vaccinating sheep

In the late 1870s and early 1880s, following his work on chicken cholera, Louis Pasteur began to investigate the possibility of making vaccines against other infectious diseases. He started with anthrax. Using Koch's laboratory techniques and his own work on chicken cholera, he was able to develop a vaccine from the anthrax microbe. His first tests in sheep were carried out successfully.

A lot of people did not believe Pasteur, however, and challenged him to prove that his vaccine worked. He agreed, and in May 1881 he set up a public demonstration. One group of sheep was injected with Pasteur's vaccine and another group was not. All of the sheep were then injected with live anthrax microbes. If Pasteur's vaccine was as good as he claimed, all the vaccinated sheep should stay healthy and all the unvaccinated sheep should die. He waited anxiously. But he did not have to worry, because the demonstration worked! His vaccine protected the sheep from anthrax.

## Developing antitoxins

Other scientists were also working on vaccine development. But some were looking for a different way of treating infectious diseases. In 1889 two scientists, Emil Adolf von Behring and Kitisato Shibasaburo, were working together in Germany. They found that they could protect animals from an infectious disease by injecting them with **serum** (the liquid part of the blood) from an infected animal. They called the serum an **antitoxin**, which means a substance that acts against a poison. They thought the method must work because the serum contained something that killed the microbes.

### ? HOW WAS DIPHTHERIA TREATED?

Diphtheria was an infectious disease that usually affected children. The lungs and airways became blocked so that the child could not breathe and often died. By injecting a diphtheria antitoxin, developed by a German scientist named Paul Ehrlich (1854–1915), the infection could be controlled and cured. This treatment saved the lives of many children.

The most important use of an antitoxin was in the fight against **diphtheria**. Antitoxins were also developed against other infectious diseases, such as tetanus.

## JOSEPH MEISTER'S STORY

In 1885 a mother begged Pasteur to save her nine-year-old son, Joseph Meister, who had been badly bitten by a rabies-infected dog. Rabies was a terrifying disease. People usually caught it when they were bitten by an animal that already had rabies. Most people who became infected with rabies died. By 1885 Pasteur had developed a rabies vaccine that worked in animals. In 1885 he had not yet tested it on humans. Nevertheless, Pasteur agreed to give the vaccine to Joseph, and the boy did not become ill with rabies. Pasteur had achieved another vaccination success!

This illustration, published in 1886, shows Louis Pasteur vaccinating a young boy against rabies.

# Preventing Infection

Louis Pasteur and Robert Koch had proved that **microbes** could cause infections. Pasteur had also proved that heat could kill microbes. A Scottish surgeon, Joseph Lister (1827–1912), used this knowledge to take the first steps toward reducing infections among patients in hospitals.

In the early 1800s, people did not know how important **hygiene**, or cleanliness, was. Doctors and nurses did not wash their hands after touching patients. Bandages and surgical instruments were not cleaned thoroughly before being used again. In fact hospitals were not particularly clean places. All this meant that infections were common and could be very easily passed from one patient to another. The result was that more people died of hospital infections than from surgery!

## Keeping hospitals clean

Joseph Lister was a surgeon at Glasgow Royal Infirmary in Scotland. He studied what happened when a wound became infected. He noticed that the skin first became red and swollen. Then **pus** oozed out of the wound. After this the patient often became feverish and died. If he could find a way of stopping this dreadful process, Lister thought he might be able to start saving his patients' lives.

Lister already knew about Pasteur's work. He knew he had to prevent the microbes in the air from reaching the wound. At first, he told his staff to cover the wound with clean bandages immediately after surgery. This helped, but it was not enough on its own.

Then he made another rule. He insisted that all medical staff wash their hands before examining each patient. In addition all surgical instruments had to be **sterilized** by heating after use. Both these measures helped. But Lister still wanted to find a way to get rid of even more microbes. He needed a substance that could be used throughout the hospital.

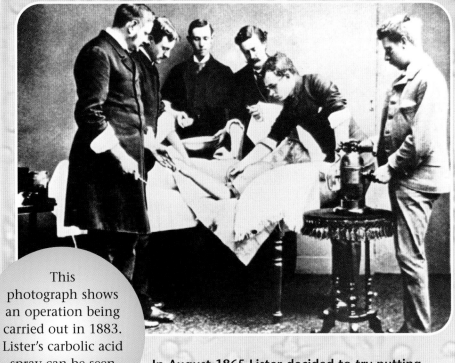

This photograph shows an operation being carried out in 1883. Lister's carbolic acid spray can be seen on the right.

In August 1865 Lister decided to try putting carbolic acid directly onto a wound. An 11-year-old boy, James Greenlees, was hurt in an accident. His leg was badly injured. Lister soaked a bandage in a mixture of linseed oil and carbolic acid. Then he put it over the wound. He covered it with tin foil to stop the bandage from drying out. The wound healed quickly, without any sign of infection.

He had heard about a chemical called carbolic acid, which had been used to prevent the spread of a disease called typhoid. Lister told his staff to wash the hospital floors with carbolic acid. He also told them to soak hospital sheets and towels in it. After this, the number of infections dropped rapidly.

Joseph Lister had begun to prevent the spread of infections in hospitals. He was the first person to use a chemical as an **antiseptic**. After this other doctors began to use his methods of preventing infection. Scientists also began to search for more chemicals that could be used instead of carbolic acid.

## Social hygiene

Although Lister's work reduced the number of infections among hospital patients, it did not solve all the problems. Many people caught infections in their homes, streets, and workplaces. What could be causing these infections?

## Dirty water?

In the mid-1800s, many doctors and other people thought that dirty water might lead to everyday infections. At that time few ordinary people had a clean, piped water supply to their homes. Most got their water from wells or pumps in the streets. There were no flushing toilets or **sewage** systems. Waste ended up in drains, streams, and rivers.

In 1854 there was a bad outbreak of cholera in London. This gave an English doctor, John Snow (1813–1858), a chance to test the dirty water theory. Cholera is an infectious disease that causes sickness, diarrhea, and often death. When John Snow investigated, he found that most of the people who died got their water from one particular pump. Few people who used other pumps or wells became infected. The local prison had its own well, and very few prisoners became ill. Nobody who worked at the local brewery became ill either. They had a free supply of beer so they did not drink any water from the pump!

Children like these in the 1800s lived in very poor conditions, with no running water.

When John Snow showed all his evidence to the authorities they removed the pump handle. This meant that nobody could use that pump and drink the infected water. When they investigated, the authorities found that the water was **contaminated** with waste from a local drain.

The dirty water theory was correct. John Snow's groundbreaking work in studying how infectious diseases spread was the beginning of the science we now know as **epidemiology**.

Similar findings were obtained elsewhere. Gradually other cities throughout Europe and the United States began to improve their water supplies and sewage systems. This led to a reduction in the number of infections and a general improvement in the health of millions of people.

This boy was photographed collecting water in Bangladesh in 1997. He was living in a refugee camp without a clean water supply or adequate sewage system. This meant that infections, such as cholera, typhoid, and dysentery, were common.

## ? HOW DOES DIRTY WATER SPREAD INFECTIONS SUCH AS CHOLERA?

Cholera causes sickness and diarrhea. The microbe that causes the cholera infection leaves the body in the infected person's waste. Without an efficient sewage system, the waste can contaminate the water supply. This means that the microbe gets into the water supply and infects other people. Their waste contaminates the water supply even more. And so the infection goes on and on. In rich countries most people have clean drinking water and efficient sewage systems. In poorer countries, though, infections from dirty water are still an everyday risk.

# Developing Medicines

Although it was helpful to know what caused infections, a vaccine or **antiseptic** was no help once a person had already caught a disease. To cure an infection, or to make a patient feel better, medicines were needed.

Most early medicines were based on old plant remedies. Leaves, roots, shoots, and flowers could be crushed. They could then be made into pastes and powders to swallow or put on the skin. But nobody understood exactly how these remedies worked.

## The start of a new industry

The study of chemistry developed rapidly at the end of the 1700s and the beginning of the 1800s. Chemists were learning to purify and identify new chemical substances. As chemists developed their skills, they found they could separate mixtures into the individual chemicals they contained. Some began to ask questions. Might the old plant remedies work because they contained special chemicals?

At the same time, other scientists were developing ways of testing chemicals accurately. They hoped that these new methods would help them find out exactly what different chemicals did inside the body.

Dried bark from the white willow tree is still used in herbal medicine to relieve pain and reduce a patient's temperature.

Early medicines were chemicals that came from plants. Now scientists wanted to make new chemicals that could be used as medicines. We can trace the story of one of the first laboratory-made medicines. Willow leaves and bark had been used as painkillers since ancient Greek times. In 1828 a few golden crystals were purified from willow bark. Scientists called this substance "salicin."

Although salicin did work as a painkiller, it also caused stomach problems. Scientists needed a chemical that had the same painkilling effect as salicin, but without the side effects. In 1853 a French chemist named Charles Gerhardt managed to make exactly that. It was a new chemical called acetylsalicylic acid. This should have been an exciting breakthrough. But Charles Gerhardt did not tell many people about it, so it was ignored for more than 30 years!

## THAT'S AMAZING!

In the early 1800s, the first pure medicines were separated from plant material. Some of these were very dangerous substances! One was strychnine, a powerful poison. This was obtained from a tree found in India. Another was morphine, a painkiller, which came from opium poppies.

Then, in the 1890s, Felix Hoffmann, a German chemist, came across Gerhardt's work. Hoffmann tested the chemical on his father, who had painful arthritis, and found that it was a wonderful painkiller. Bayer, the company Hoffmann worked for, began to make the chemical in large quantities. They sold it to the public under a new name: aspirin.

A sign advertising Bayer aspirin can be seen in the window of this drug store in Flemington, New Jersey, in 1935.

## Magic bullets

Chemists learned how to make, separate, and purify a wide range of new chemicals in the laboratory. Might any of these newly produced chemicals be useful in fighting the battle against infectious diseases?

Paul Ehrlich studied medicine in Germany. While he was at college, he did some research on **cells**. Cells are the smallest possible living units. All living things are made up of one or more cells. Ehrlich learned how to stain cells with chemical dyes. Interestingly, different chemicals stained different cells, or they stained different structures within cells.

After carrying out other research, including developing the **antitoxin** for **diphtheria** (see page 20), Ehrlich turned his attention back to the chemical dyes. He began to ask himself a number of questions:

● If chemical dyes were attracted to some cells, but not others, might other chemicals behave like this, too?

● If they did, might certain chemicals be attracted to diseased or infected cells, but not attracted to healthy ones?

● And might there be chemicals that would kill **microbes,** but not healthy cells?

In order to find answers to his questions, Paul Ehrlich carried out some experiments. He wanted to find chemicals that would specifically target and kill disease-causing microbes. He thought of a memorable name for these chemicals. He called them "magic bullets."

Ehrlich thought he might find his magic bullets among the new laboratory-made chemicals. He began with a disease called **sleeping sickness**, which has always been common in African countries. Ehrlich looked for a chemical that would kill the microbes that caused this disease. He tried different chemicals made from coal tar dyes. Then he tried others containing arsenic and benzene, but without much success.

## Number 606

Ehrlich did not give up. Instead, he decided to look for a chemical that would kill a different microbe. He chose the microbe that caused syphilis. This was an infectious disease that affected people all over the world. He began to test even more chemicals. Out of hundreds of different substances, one, which he had labeled number 606, seemed to work. Ehrlich and his assistants repeated their experiments. All their tests showed that the substance numbered 606 really did kill the syphilis microbe. Even better, it did this without harming other cells. Ehrlich had found his first magic bullet!

Ehrlich gave number 606 the name Salvarsan. He then announced his discovery to the world. Thanks to the work of Paul Ehrlich and his assistants, syphilis could now be cured. This was the beginning of modern chemotherapy.

## WHAT IS CHEMOTHERAPY?

Chemotherapy means using specific medicines to cure specific diseases. The disease must be identified, rather than just the symptoms. For example, **pneumonia** and food poisoning can both cause fevers, but a different medicine is used to treat each illness. The term chemotherapy really covers all the medicines that can be used to treat illnesses. However, most people only associate chemotherapy with the strong drugs used to treat many forms of cancer.

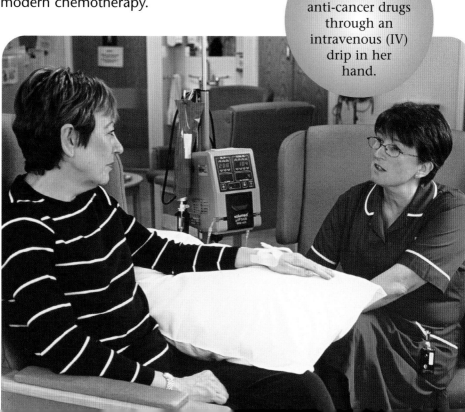

This patient is receiving anti-cancer drugs through an intravenous (IV) drip in her hand.

# Killing Microbes

In 1928 there was a discovery that would revolutionize the fight against infectious diseases. **Penicillin**, the first **antibiotic**, was discovered. But this breakthrough was not made because of a carefully planned scientific investigation. It was the result of a rather lucky accident!

## THAT'S AMAZING!

Alexander Fleming was not the first scientist to notice the microbe-killing properties of some molds. This breakthrough had actually been made in 1897 by a French medical student named Ernest Duschesne. But, because Duchesne's work had never been published, other scientists did not get to hear about it!

Alexander Fleming (1881–1955) had studied medicine and then became a medical researcher. Like many other scientists at the time, his aim was to find Paul Ehrlich's magic bullets (see pages 28–29). Fleming spent several years investigating liquids, such as tears and saliva. He found that these contained **lysozyme**, a chemical that made **microbes** burst open. Fleming isolated and purified lysozyme. He then did some experiments to test how effective lysozyme would be at killing different microbes.

Sir Alexander Fleming, the pioneering Scottish scientist, in 1944.

## Moldy dishes

In 1928 Fleming went away for a few days, leaving **cultures** of microbes growing in a nutrient mixture. He intended to use them in his lysozyme experiments. When he came back, he examined his cultures and got a surprise. In one dish a colony of microbes had begun to grow and had then died. Strangely, a patch of mold had grown in the same dish. Could the mold have produced a chemical that killed the microbes? If so this might be the very chemical he had been searching for.

Fleming grew some more of the mold. Then he took the nutrient mixture the mold had grown in. He separated and purified all the chemicals the mixture contained. Among these was a chemical that had not been in the original nutrient mixture. This must have been produced by the mold. When Fleming tested this chemical, he found that it really did kill microbes.

Fleming called his new chemical penicillin, because it was made by a mold named *Penicillium notatum*. But things did not progress smoothly after that. No matter how hard Fleming tried, he could not obtain enough pure penicillin to take his tests any further. Frustrated, he gave up his work on penicillin. Luckily, though, this was not the end of the story.

This illustration shows Fleming's notes and his drawing of the original culture plate of the mold *Penicillium notatum*.

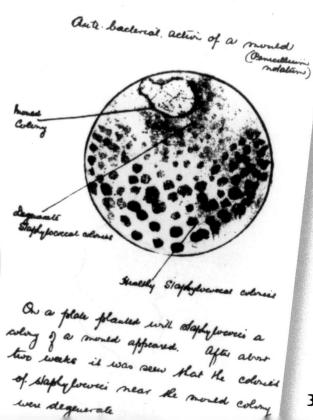

31

## The next step for penicillin

After penicillin's antibiotic activity had been announced by Alexander Fleming in 1929, it was ignored for several years. In 1937 two scientists working in Oxford, in the United Kingdom, began to look at penicillin again. These scientists were Howard Florey, an Australian, and Ernst Boris Chain, a German.

At first Florey and Chain came up against the same problems as Fleming. Although they could grow the mold, they could not isolate and purify penicillin. Then, after many failed attempts, Chain tried a new technique called freeze-drying. This stabilized the penicillin and stopped it from breaking down. Freeze-drying is common now and is used in processes such as producing instant coffee. But in the late 1930s, when Florey and Chain were working, it was still very new. Nevertheless it worked! Chain produced enough penicillin to enable the two scientists to carry out more tests.

U.S. Army doctors operate on a wounded soldier near the front line, in Italy, in 1944. Before penicillin became available, many soldiers died from infected wounds.

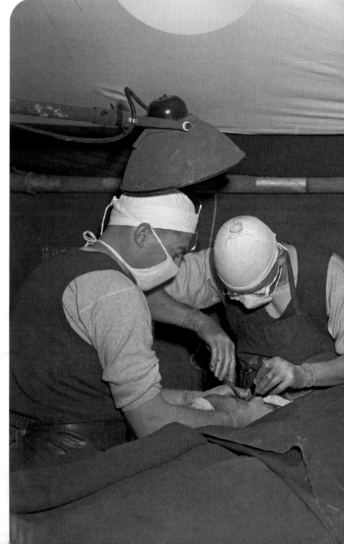

## Testing pencillin

In May 1940 penicillin was tested in mice. Two groups of mice were given shots of a microbe that would normally kill them. One group was given several penicillin shots. The other group had no treatment at all. The results were very clear. All the mice who had received penicillin recovered, but all the untreated mice died.

In any war many soldiers get wounded. Without quick treatment, these wounds soon become infected. Before penicillin was available, many soldiers died from infections. The large-scale production of penicillin in the United States meant that doctors could treat infections. This saved the lives of many American and British soldiers during World War II (1939–1945). There was even enough penicillin to treat many civilians, too.

The next step was to test penicillin in humans. Early test results were encouraging. They showed that penicillin could cure infections in people, without doing any major harm. But, although there was enough penicillin for a few tests, there was not enough to treat large numbers of patients.

Now Howard Florey turned to the Rockefeller Foundation in New York for help. The Rockefeller Foundation was a charity that had been set up in 1913 specifically to "promote the well-being of mankind throughout the world." It had a lot of money and could provide financial support for causes that it thought were worthwhile. Drug companies were persuaded to become involved and, together, they could make large quantities of penicillin. At last there was a drug that would successfully cure some infectious diseases in humans. In 1945 Fleming, Florey, and Chain were jointly awarded a Nobel Prize for their work on penicillin.

## Searching for other antibiotics

During the 1930s, in Germany, a scientist named Gerhard Domagk (1895–1964) was searching for antibiotics that would kill microbes in humans without hurting the patient in any way. Any problems caused by a medicine, such as a rash or a feeling of sickness, are called side effects.

Following Paul Ehrlich's work (see pages 28–29), Domagk decided to concentrate on looking at chemical dyes. He thought that a red dye, which he named Prontosil, might be able to kill microbes. Tests on mice proved that he was right. Prontosil could cure infections.

Gerhard Domagk won the Nobel Prize in 1939, but Adolf Hitler, leader of the Nazi Party, would not let him accept it. He finally received his medal after the war, in 1947.

## The first sulfa drugs

However, there was a puzzle about Prontosil. Although it worked in mice, it would not kill microbes in a test tube. Domagk wanted to find out why. But two French scientists, Jacques and Therese Trefouel, solved the puzzle first. They showed that Prontosil was split into two different chemicals in the body. One of these, sulfonamide, killed microbes, but the other chemical did not. Prontosil did not work in a test tube because it did not get split up.

## HILDEGAARD DOMAGK'S STORY

Domagk first tested Prontosil on his youngest daughter, Hildegaard. She had pricked her finger with a needle and the wound had become infected. The infection spread throughout her body and she was so ill the doctors were sure she would die. Domagk was desperate to save her life. Trying Prontosil seemed to be his only hope. He gave the drug to Hildegaard and she soon made a full recovery!

*"The problem of chemotherapy of bacterial infections could be solved neither by the experimental medical research worker nor by the chemist alone, but only by the two together working in very close co-operation over many years."*
From Domagk's Nobel Prize lecture, December 12, 1947

Sulfonamide was isolated and purified. The pure chemical was then tested on its own. It seemed to kill some microbes, but not others. This meant that it could cure some, but not all, infections. It was the first of a group of medicines that became known as the sulfa drugs.

A year later, another sulfa drug, sulfapyridine, was made in the laboratory. More sulfa drugs followed, but none was as successful as penicillin. This was because, although the sulfa drugs did cure some infections, they also had unpleasant side effects. They affected the blood, so patients looked blue. They also often damaged the patient's own resistance to infections.

This is a model of a sulfonamide **molecule**. The carbon atoms are black, hydrogen are white, nitrogen are blue, oxygen are red, and sulphur is yellow.

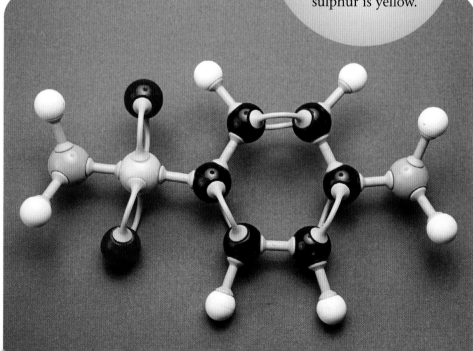

## Finding a cure for tuberculosis

**Tuberculosis (TB)** is a very serious infectious disease that affects the lungs. It also used to be known as consumption. In the early 1900s, it mainly affected children and young adults. Because few people recovered from it, people were very afraid of catching it. Many people used to die from TB every year, and it could not be cured by penicillin. Scientists searching for microbe-killing chemicals were therefore anxious to find a cure for this disease.

In the United States, a Ukrainian scientist named Selman Waksman was studying soil. He tested mold and other soil organisms, searching for any that produced microbe-killing chemicals. In 1940 Waksman and his team discovered a chemical that looked promising. Because it was produced by soil organisms called actinomycetes, Waksman called his chemical actinomycin. Waksman tested actinomycin in animals. Although it did cure infections, it also caused other damage. Actinomycin was not going to be suitable for use in humans.

## A new microbe-killer

Waksman was very disappointed, but carried on with his research. Three years later, one of his students, Albert Schatz, discovered another chemical made by soil organisms called streptomycetes. He called the chemical streptomycin and told Waksman about it. Together, Waksman, Schatz, and other scientists in the team tested streptomycin. All the test results proved that streptomycin killed microbes. Even better, it killed microbes that penicillin did not!

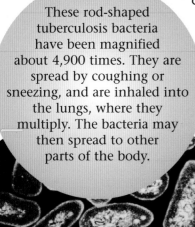

These rod-shaped tuberculosis bacteria have been magnified about 4,900 times. They are spread by coughing or sneezing, and are inhaled into the lungs, where they multiply. The bacteria may then spread to other parts of the body.

Merck, a large drug company in the United States, began mass-producing streptomycin. Major tests on people began in 1944 and were very successful. Streptomycin did cause dizziness and sickness in some patients. These side effects were not serious, though, compared with the infections the drug could cure. Probably the most important fact about streptomycin was that it could cure tuberculosis. Until then there had been no cure for this deadly infectious disease.

Waksman received all the praise and fame for the discovery of streptomycin. Schatz's part in the discovery was almost forgotten. Some people thought this was justified because Waksman was in charge of the students and all the work that went on in his department. But others thought it was unfair and believed that Schatz deserved some recognition.

## HOW DID DOCTORS TREAT TB?

Before the 1940s doctors advised TB patients to get plenty of rest. Some patients were sent to places with clean mountain air. A vaccine had also been developed, but there was no real cure. Today, thanks to streptomycin and other modern medicines, TB is not a common disease in developed countries. However, it is still very common in parts of the world where modern medicine is not easily available.

A TB clinic was known as a sanatorium. These young girls were photographed in a sanatorium in the French Alps, in 1933. They had been sent there because it was hoped that the mountain air would help cure them.

# Modern Vaccines

Following the early work on vaccines and **antitoxins**, teams of scientists continued the search for vaccines to protect people against other infectious diseases. However, before they could really progress, they needed to know more about how the body reacts to **microbes**. Progress in many areas of medicine was hampered by infections. But, without knowing how the body reacted when microbes entered it, scientists could not understand how vaccines and antitoxins worked. They needed a way of seeing tiny microbes, such as **viruses**, and a technique that would enable them to grow viruses in the laboratory.

A scientist uses an early electron microscope in 1949.

Back in the 1800s, Paul Ehrlich had studied infectious diseases for many years. In the 1890s, he put forward a theory to explain how the body reacts to a microbe. He suggested that the first time a microbe enters the body, the body produces chemicals to fight it. The body somehow remembers the microbe. Then, if the same microbe enters again, the body can react quickly to prevent an infection from developing. This was the first explanation of how the **immune system** worked. Ehrlich was convinced that this also explained how vaccines and antitoxins worked.

## Putting microbes under the microscope

By the end of the 1800s, some microbes had been trapped in special filters. They were then observed under a microscope, described, and named. These included the microbes that cause diseases such as cholera. But scientists realized that some microbes were too small to be trapped in even the finest filters. This made it very difficult to study them.

Then there were two major breakthroughs. First, in 1907, a British scientist named R.G. Harrison developed a way of growing animal **cells** in the laboratory. This technique was called tissue culture. For the first time, scientists could grow these tiny microbes inside animal cells and study them. Second, the invention of the electron microscope in the 1930s allowed scientists to observe these very tiny microbes. They were called viruses.

By the end of the 1930s, scientists had three new things to help them in their work:

**1.** ideas about how the body reacts to microbes

**2.** a technique for growing viruses

**3.** an instrument that allowed them to see viruses and other microbes.

They could now take the next step on the path toward developing new vaccines.

This photograph of human red blood cells and a single white blood cell, magnified around 650 times, shows the amazing level of detail provided by an electron microscope.

## HOW DO ANTITOXINS AND VACCINES WORK?

● An antitoxin contains the chemicals produced by one individual to fight a particular microbe. When the antitoxin is injected into an infected individual, the chemicals help the injected individual's defense system fight the microbe. This cures the infection.

● A vaccine works by introducing a weak or dead microbe to the body's defense system. The body produces chemicals to fight the microbe and remembers it. Then, whenever a live microbe enters the body, the defense system reacts quickly and prevents an infection from developing.

## Polio

Following the advances of the 1920s and 1930s, several vaccines were introduced. These included the BCG vaccine for tuberculosis. Then a vaccine against **polio** was developed.

Poliomyelitis, usually called polio, is an infectious disease that mainly affects children. It attacks the nerves, causing paralysis and often death. Many children used to be crippled by polio. They needed crutches or metal supports for their legs to help them walk. Others spent months or even years in machines called "iron lungs." This was because polio had paralyzed their chest muscles and they found it difficult to breathe without help.

In 1947 an American scientist, Jonas Salk, began to search for a polio vaccine. Scientists had already found more than a hundred different versions of the polio virus. But Salk found that these could all be sorted into three main groups. Any vaccine had to offer protection against viruses from each of these three groups.

## Growing viruses

At first, it was difficult to get enough virus material to work with. Then, in 1948, a team of three scientists named J.F. Enders, T.H. Weller, and F.C. Robbins found a way of growing large quantities of virus. They found that viruses would multiply inside fertilized chicken eggs. By treating the eggs with **penicillin**, they could stop **contamination** by other microbes. In this way, they grew mumps viruses in their laboratory. They then used this technique to grow viruses, including polio.

### IS THERE AN ALTERNATIVE POLIO VACCINE?

Another scientist, Albert Sabin, thought the polio vaccine should be made from weakened, but not dead, virus. He was sure this would make it more effective. He also decided to **vaccinate** people by putting the vaccine on sugar cubes so that they could swallow it. This was much easier, quicker, and cheaper than Salk's injected vaccine. Today, both Salk's and Sabin's vaccines are available for use.

Salk killed the polio virus with a chemical called formaldehyde. Once it was dead, the virus could not cause an infection. If he injected the dead virus into a person, he hoped it would make their body's immune system react and remember it.

In 1952 Salk tested his vaccine on himself, his family, and other volunteers. None of them became ill, but tests showed that their bodies had all reacted to the vaccine. This meant that they would be protected against any future infection.

Salk published his research in 1953. The next year children all over the United States were successfully vaccinated against polio. In 1952 more than 21,000 cases of polio had been reported in the United States. By the end of the 1950s, fewer than 10 cases were reported in a year.

This photograph shows people lining up outside a polio vaccination center in Texas in 1962. Mass vaccination programs have almost wiped out polio in the developed world. However, the disease is still a public health problem in developing countries.

# Vaccine production

As the demand for vaccines has increased, production methods have had to change in order to produce enough doses. Modern technology has helped to make vaccine production safe and efficient.

Producing a vaccine is a slow process. There are six main stages, described below:

**Stage 1:** The target microbe has to be grown in containers called **culture** vessels. Once enough microbes have grown, they are killed, changed, or weakened so that they cannot cause an infection. They may also be split up, so that one part can be isolated and purified. This microbe material is then mixed with other chemicals. This is the raw material for the vaccine.

**Stage 2:** Each batch of vaccine material must be carefully tested. Scientists must make sure that each batch:

- is effective against the intended microbe
- is strong enough
- is not contaminated
- contains the right amount of all the ingredients.

**Stage 3:** If the vaccine is going to offer protection against more than one infectious disease, it must then be mixed with another vaccine (or vaccines). For example, measles, mumps, and rubella vaccines are mixed together to make the MMR vaccine. This vaccine protects the person against all three of these diseases.

**Stage 4:** The vaccine is sent to government scientists for testing.

**Stage 5:** The vaccine is put into small containers, such as tiny bottles or syringes, that each hold a single dose.

**Stage 6:** The vaccine doses are packaged. They are then ready to be sent out to hospitals and doctors.

## Giving vaccines

Early vaccinations were given using reusable glass syringes and metal needles. In 1954 the first **sterile** glass disposable syringe was introduced. This made distributing Salk's polio vaccine much easier. Soon afterward, a cheaper plastic version was developed. In recent years many of the large pharmaceutical companies have tried to find better methods of giving vaccines. One is a micro-needle, a pre-filled syringe that has a tiny needle no thicker than a hair! Another is a needle-free device, which uses carbon dioxide to force the vaccine under the skin.

This photograph shows children being vaccinated in Kenya in 2000. Large-scale vaccination programs such as this can save many lives.

## ? CAN A DISEASE BE COMPLETELY WIPED OUT?

If enough people in the world can be vaccinated against a disease, the disease will die out. This is because there are not enough people for the disease to spread to. This has happened with **smallpox**. If enough vaccine doses can be distributed to places where diseases such as tuberculosis are common, doctors hope that these diseases will also eventually die out. However, this is difficult to achieve because vaccines can be expensive. In addition not all governments wish to pay for the required medical staff and transport.

# Modern Antibiotics

After the success of **penicillin** and streptomycin in fighting infections, some scientists searched for more **antibiotics** in the soil. Other researchers found different ways of changing existing antibiotics, and even producing new antibiotics in the laboratory.

Many scientists decided to search soil for more antibiotics. Soil organisms, mainly fungi, were isolated from soil samples taken from all over the world. Researchers grew these organisms in the laboratory. The chemicals they produced were tested for antibiotic activity. Any chemicals shown to kill **microbes** were then tested in animals.

In the 1950s some tourists brought soil samples back from other countries.

In the 1950s travel was expensive and journeys took longer than they do today. Instead of sending scientists on special trips, drug companies got other people to help. They persuaded people who were already going to travel, such as airline pilots, soldiers, and vacationers, to collect soil samples for them!

Although many antibiotic chemicals were found in this way, they often caused such serious side effects that they were not studied any further. Some of the most successful ones include aureomycin and terramycin. These were particularly useful because they attacked a wider range of microbes than earlier antibiotics. Doctors and scientists therefore referred to them as broad-spectrum antibiotics.

Lloyd H. Conover was a chemist who worked for the drug company Pfizer. He noticed that the centers of the terramycin and aureomycin **molecules** were identical. They were made up of a group of atoms that did not change. He called this group tetracycline. Pfizer **patented** tetracycline in 1955, and this led to the production of a whole new range of antibiotics. Each of the new antibiotics had a tetracycline group at the center of its molecule.

There is now a wide range of antibiotic pills, tablets, and capsules available.

Scientists found that penicillin also had a central group of atoms. They called this beta-lactam. By keeping beta-lactam at the center, but changing other parts of the penicillin molecule, they could produce completely new antibiotics. Some, such as ampicillin and amoxicillin, were even better than penicillin because they could be used to treat an even wider range of infections.

## ? HOW DO ANTIBIOTICS FIGHT INFECTIONS?

There are three main ways in which antibiotics fight infections:

1. They stop microbes from making new **cell** wall materials. As the cell walls become weak, they cannot be mended. The microbes eventually burst open and die. The penicillin family of antibiotics works in this way.

2. They prevent the microbe from reproducing. If no more microbes are produced, the body's own defenses can control the infection and destroy any remaining microbes. The sulfa drugs act in this way.

3. They prevent **proteins** from being made inside the microbe. This stops the microbes from functioning properly and eventually kills them. Streptomycin acts in this way.

## Antibiotic production

In the early days of antibiotic research, a single scientist or a small group of people did all the work. Now, drug companies employ large teams of scientists to do their research on new medicines. In addition powerful computers and robotic machinery mean that far more chemicals can be tested than was previously possible.

Starting with the structures of known antibiotics, scientists use computer-modeling techniques to recognize structures of other molecules that might also be antibiotics. The computer models can also compare these with other chemicals, and help eliminate any that are likely to cause side effects in patients. This leaves the scientists with a smaller number of chemicals to test.

At first tests are carried out in **cultures** of cells in the laboratory. After that, the chemicals may be tested on animals. This is to check that the chemical does actually work as an antibiotic and also that it does not cause side effects. Only after all these stages have been completed can the chemical be tested on humans. Once a chemical has been found to have antibiotic activity and to be safe to use as a medicine, mass production can begin.

This scientist is carrying out antibiotic research for a biotechnology company.

Many antibiotics are produced by minute organisms grown in huge containers called **fermentation** tanks. A liquid containing all the nutrients the microorganisms need for growth is put into the tanks.

The container and its contents have to be monitored all the time. The oxygen level, temperature, and nutrient levels have to be kept exactly right. This is all controlled by computers.

As the microorganisms grow, the antibiotics are produced. When the microorganisms have finished growing, they die. The mixture is filtered, and the antibiotic is isolated and purified.

Some antibiotics are not made by microorganisms. Instead they are produced in the laboratory from chemicals. When a large enough quantity of the antibiotic is ready, it is purified and can move on to the next stage.

## Ready for use

The pure antibiotic is made into whatever form is needed. Antibiotics that are to be swallowed are made into tablets or capsules. Antibiotics that are to be given by injection are mixed to the correct strength with liquids and put into tiny single-dose bottles or syringes.

Tests must be carried out at every stage to ensure that the final product is absolutely safe for use as a medicine. As with vaccines, some tests are carried out by government scientists to make sure that all the correct standards are met.

A worker inspects the huge fermentation tanks in the production hall of a pharmaceutical factory. The antibiotic being produced is penicillin.

# Preventing Infection Today

Since the end of the 1800s, advances in healthcare and **hygiene** have greatly reduced the number of infections that occur. Many people can see these advances in their everyday lives.

During the last hundred years, living conditions in many parts of the world have changed dramatically. The changes have been gradual, and they have affected whole societies. However, these changes have only come about in the developed world. In some other parts of the world, living conditions are still very poor and infections still rage, claiming many lives every year. People living in these less developed areas would benefit enormously if similar changes could be made in their own societies.

One important change in the developed world is that most houses now have a clean water supply. This means that water is safe for drinking and cooking. With access to clean water, people can keep themselves, their belongings, and their surroundings clean and infection-free.

During the rainy season, slum villages in the Philippines often get swamped in their own sewage. This can lead to widespread disease.

In the developed world, most houses also have sanitation systems that remove **sewage** and waste from the house. This ensures that such waste does not **contaminate** other people, food, or water supplies. Infections from such waste are therefore unlikely to occur. In addition, in these countries, garbage is collected regularly, before it rots. Again this reduces the risk of infections and disease.

In the developed world, a reliable electricity supply allows people to store food in fridges and freezers. Together with improved production methods and modern packaging, refrigeration enables people to keep their food fresh for longer. The number of infections arising from food is therefore reduced. In many parts of the world, though, electricity is expensive or unavailable. Here other energy sources, such as solar power, can sometimes be used to power fridges and freezers.

Making clean water, sanitation, and power supplies available to all communities is not enough, however. Along with these improvements, people need access to good healthcare and education. Without reliable medical treatment and information, new scientific discoveries can make little difference to public health.

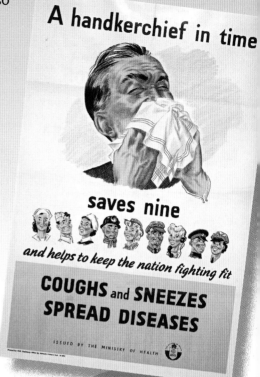

A handkerchief in time saves nine

and helps to keep the nation fighting fit

**COUGHS and SNEEZES SPREAD DISEASES**

ISSUED BY THE MINISTRY OF HEALTH

During World War II (1939–1945), governments used posters like this one to educate people about health risks.

## ? HOW CAN EDUCATION IMPROVE HEALTH?

Coughing, sneezing, and spitting all release germs that can infect others. Thanks to education campaigns, people are now more aware of this than they used to be. They know that simple things, such as covering their mouths when they cough, sneezing into a tissue or handkerchief, or washing their hands after using the bathroom, can all reduce the risk of spreading infections.

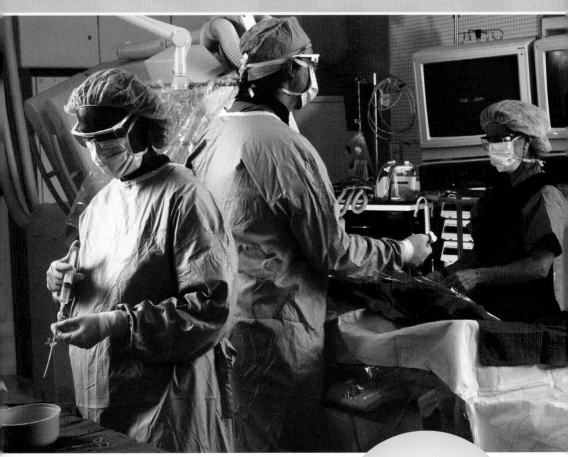

## Preventing infections in hospitals

Our hospitals have changed a lot since the end of the 1800s. If you go to a health center or hospital today, you will usually see how carefully people follow the rules of good hygiene. Modern equipment and medical training enable staff to treat a much wider range of illnesses. However, without the earlier discoveries of scientists such as Koch and Lister, none of these important advances would have been possible.

Preventing infections is important at every stage of a patient's treatment during their stay in the hospital. An infection puts the individual patient's life in danger. It also puts other patients, visitors, staff, and even the general community at risk.

A surgeon and some nurses are seen here at work in a sterile operating room. Their caps, masks, and gloves all help to protect the patient against infection.

The discoveries you have read about mean that if you go into the hospital you will notice that:

- hospital wards are clean and neat

- there are high general standards of cleanliness

- equipment and furniture are designed so that it is easy to keep them clean

- sheets and towels are washed regularly

- nurses and other hospital staff wear clean uniforms

- patients are encouraged to keep up high standards of personal hygiene.

In addition reusable instruments in operating rooms are **sterilized** after use. Many other items, such as needles and syringes, are **sterile** when packed. They are used once and are then thrown away. Bandages are all sterile before use. Doctors and assisting staff wear clean surgical gowns, masks, gloves, and hats in operating rooms. These measures all help ensure that patients' wounds do not become infected during their surgeries.

**Antiseptic** soaps and scrubs are available for hand washing so that infections are not passed from person to person. Antiseptic sprays, wipes, and bandages all help keep wounds infection-free. Some patients are given **antibiotics** before, or immediately after, an operation to prevent any possible infection from developing. Other patients may receive antibiotics if there are signs that they have an infection. In these cases the antibiotics should prevent the infection from getting worse. Finally, if a person is suspected of having a particularly dangerous infection, they may be isolated to prevent it from spreading to anybody else.

These measures have greatly reduced infections in hospitals. However, despite all the modern antiseptics and hygiene procedures, serious infections still occur.

TALKING SCIENCE

*"Infections acquired in hospitals and healthcare institutions affect approximately 2 million people, resulting in about 98,000 deaths at a cost of $29 billion in the United States each year."*
Joseph Cervia, MD, Professor of Clinical Medicine and Pediatrics at Albert Einstein College of Medicine in New York, and Medical Director of Pall Corporation

# Current Research

However successful previous research has been, scientists never stop looking for new and better chemicals, techniques, and solutions to problems. Also the problems themselves keep changing, so research must continue in order to keep up.

One of the biggest problems today is that, over time, **microbes** can develop a resistance to particular **antibiotics**. This means that an antibiotic that previously killed a particular microbe can no longer do so. Scientists then need to find a new antibiotic that will kill the new version of the microbe. This has become an increasingly serious problem.

## WHAT IS MRSA?

One example of an antibiotic-resistant microbe is MRSA. This stands for **m**ethicillin-**r**esistant *Staphylococcus* **a***ureus*. Old strains of the microbe *Staphyloccus aureus* could be killed by an antibiotic called methicillin. But methicillin is useless against the newer strains that have developed. Although MRSA is not serious for healthy people, it can be dangerous for patients in hospitals who are already sick or weak.

These researchers are looking for organisms that can be used to manufacture new pharmaceutical drugs. They are using a net to collect samples of plankton from a coastal mangrove swamp in Mozambique, Africa.

## Back to old remedies

Scientists today are investigating some amazing natural sources of antibiotics. These sources include crocodile blood, seaweed, frog skin, and soya beans! In 2000 an antibiotic called "crocodillin" was discovered in crocodile blood. And in 2005 antibiotic activity was detected in Scottish seaweed.

Many native peoples use traditional remedies, and these are often obtained from plants. Some of these plants have been tested and found to contain certain chemicals. These chemicals sometimes prove to be valuable medicines. Tea tree oil is one example of an infection-fighting substance developed from a traditional remedy. Tea tree oil was used for cleaning cuts and other minor injuries for many years. But when modern **antiseptics** and other new medicines were introduced, old remedies such as this one fell out of everyday use. Now scientists hope they will prove useful in the battle against antibiotic-resistant microbes.

## Space age science

Antibiotic research is also being carried out in space! Experiments on the space shuttle and space station have shown that some microorganisms can produce much greater quantities of antibiotic in space than they do on Earth. At present there is no plan to produce antibiotics on a large scale in space. But scientists are excited about investigating the reasons for this increase in production. Once they have found out why the microorganisms react in this way, they may be able to improve their methods of producing antibiotics on Earth.

## TALKING SCIENCE

*"More than 70 percent of the bacteria that cause hospital-acquired infections are resistant to at least one of the drugs most commonly used to treat them. Persons infected with drug-resistant organisms are more likely to have longer hospital stays and require treatment with second or third choice drugs that may be less effective, more toxic, and more expensive."*
Centers for Disease Control and Prevention (CDC)

## New vaccines

Many more infectious diseases could be prevented if suitable vaccines were available. One of today's main challenges is to find a vaccine for **HIV (Human Immunodeficiency Virus)**. This virus causes the illness known as **AIDS (Acquired Immune Deficiency Syndrome)**, which kills millions of people every year. Vaccines against other infectious diseases, such as malaria, are also being tested.

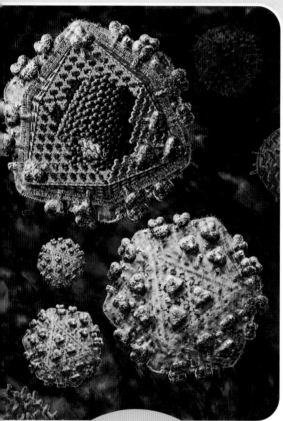

New ways of using vaccines are being investigated. "Therapeutic vaccines" are not designed to prevent infection. Instead they make a patient's own body fight illnesses they already have. Therapeutic vaccines are being developed against diseases such as type 1 diabetes and multiple sclerosis.

## Other challenges

Some types of cancer are known to arise as a result of a virus. One example is cervical cancer. In many women this is caused by infection with Human Papilloma Virus (HPV). Scientists have developed a vaccine against HPV. If this vaccine was made available to all young women, cervical cancer might one day become a very rare disease.

This illustration shows the AIDS virus. It attacks white blood cells, which play an important role in the **immune system**. This allows normally harmless infections to become life-threatening.

One of the main problems is that some viruses have many different strains, and each of these strains can keep changing! Even a tiny change in a virus can mean that a vaccine no longer offers protection against it. Influenza (flu) is like this. Each year, a different strain spreads. This is why a vaccine that offers protection one year will probably not be effective against the next year's strain. Scientists have to work quickly to produce new vaccines each time a new strain appears.

Although **allergies** are not caused by viruses, scientists think vaccines may still be able to help people who are allergic. In many people an allergy causes mild symptoms. In other people, though, an allergic reaction can be very serious. In extreme cases they may collapse or even die. Scientists are trying to develop a vaccine that will prevent these people from reacting to the things they are allergic to. This could enable them to avoid suffering dangerous allergic reactions.

By following the story of the scientific and medical discoveries discussed in this book, you can see how each has been just a small link in a long chain. Some have helped us to understand more about infectious diseases and how our bodies respond to them. Others have led to the development of the many medicines now available to us. One discovery leads to another, which leads to another, and so on. Whatever today's scientists discover will form the next link in the chain.

A nurse vaccinates a patient against flu and hepatitis A. Both flu and hepatitis A are viral infections.

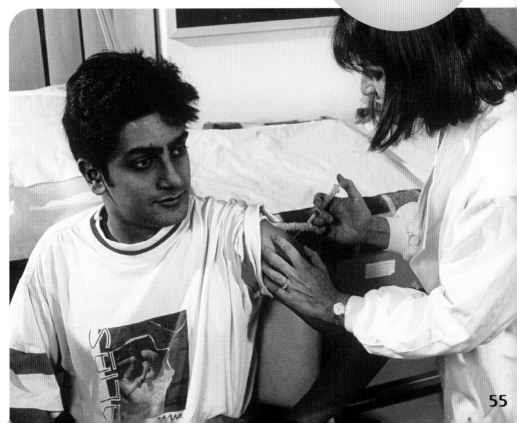

# Timeline

**400 B.C.** Scientific study of medicine begun by Hippocrates of Cos.

**100s A.D.** Important medical ideas established by Galen.

**Early 1000s** Medical ideas developed by Avicenna.

**Early 1500s** Paracelsus pioneers use of minerals.

**1796** First vaccination carried out by Edward Jenner.

**1828** Salicin extracted from willow plant material.

**1853** Charles Gerhardt synthesizes acetylsalicylic acid.

**1854** Dirty water identified by John Snow as cause of cholera outbreak in London.

**1865** Carbolic acid first used as antiseptic on wound by Joseph Lister.

**1870s** Louis Pasteur and Robert Koch establish Germ Theory.

**1881** Anthrax vaccine demonstrated in sheep by Pasteur.

**1886** First rabies vaccination in humans by Pasteur.

**1880s** Use of antitoxins pioneered by Emil Adolf von Behring.

**1889** Diphtheria antitoxin developed by Paul Ehrlich.

**1890s** Aspirin developed by Felix Hoffmann, working for Bayer.

**1907** Tissue culture technique for growing animal cells developed by R.G. Harrison.

**1928** Antibiotic action of penicillin discovered by Alexander Fleming.

**1932** Antibiotic activity of sulfa drugs discovered by Gerhard Domagk.

**1930s** Invention of electron microscope.

**1940** Actinomycin discovered by Selman Waksman and his team.

**1943** Commercial production of penicillin begins.

**1943** Streptomycin discovered by Waksman and Albert Schatz.

**1948** Method for growing large quantities of virus developed by J.F. Enders, T.H. Weller, and F.C. Robbins.

**1952** First polio vaccine developed by Jonas Salk.

**1954** First large-scale polio vaccination program in United States.

**1954** First glass disposable syringe is developed.

**1955** Tetracycline structure is identified.

**1957** Alternative polio vaccine developed by Albert Sabin.

**1960** Methicillin introduced to treat bacterial infections.

**1961** MRSA reported.

**1961** Ampicillin introduced to treat bacterial infections.

**1964** Measles vaccine introduced.

**1967** Mumps vaccine introduced.

**1970** Rubella (German measles) vaccine introduced.

**1972** Amoxicillin introduced to treat bacterial infections.

**1974** Chickenpox vaccine is introduced.

**1977** Last naturally occurring case of smallpox.

**1977** Pneumonia vaccine is introduced.

**1978** Meningitis vaccine is introduced.

**1980** World Health Organization declares smallpox officially eradicated worldwide.

**1981** Vaccine against hepatitis B is introduced.

**1983** HIV identified.

**1986** Antibiotic "magainin" discovered in frog skin.

**1988** MMR (measles, mumps, and rubella) vaccine introduced.

**1995** Vaccine against hepatitis A is introduced.

**1998** Actinomycin research carried out on space shuttle.

**2000** Antibiotic "crocodillin" is discovered in crocodile blood.

**2005** Antibiotic "plectasin" discovered in a pine forest fungus.

**2005** Antibiotic activity discovered in Scottish seaweed.

# Biographies

These are some of the leading scientists in the story of medicines.

## Paul Ehrlich (1854–1915)

Paul Ehrlich was born in Silesia, an area of Europe on the borders of Germany, Poland, and the Czech Republic. His family was Jewish. Paul went to school in Breslau and then studied medicine at several universities, including Breslau and Leipzig. He married Hedwin Pinkus in 1883 and they had two daughters. His work made him famous and he received honors from many universities across the world. He was awarded the Nobel Prize for Physiology or Medicine in 1908. Ehrlich suffered a stroke in 1914. He died in 1915, at Bad Homburg, Germany.

## Alexander Fleming (1881–1955)

Alexander Fleming was born in Lochfield, Scotland. He was one of eight children and his family were farmers. Alexander and some of his family moved to London, England when he was 14 years old. He studied medicine at London University. He served in the Royal Army Medical Corps during World War I. In 1915 he married Sarah Marion McElroy and they had one son. When the war finished, Fleming carried out research at London University. Alexander Fleming was knighted in 1944. He shared the Nobel Prize for Physiology or Medicine with Chain and Florey in 1945. His wife died in 1949, and in 1953 he married a colleague, Dr. Amalia Koutsouri-Voureka. Fleming died in 1955 and is buried in St. Paul's Cathedral, London.

## Edward Jenner (1749–1823)

Edward Jenner was born in Berkeley, Gloucestershire, England, in 1749. His parents both died when Edward was young, and he was brought up by his older brother. He went to the local village school and then to a grammar school in Cirencester. He was interested in the countryside, and spent much of his spare time finding out about local plants, animals, and fossils. After leaving school Jenner went to London to study medicine. His first job was as a doctor back in Berkeley, his home town. He married Catherine Kingscote in 1788, and they had three children. Catherine died in 1815, from tuberculosis. Jenner died after a stroke in 1823. He was buried in Berkeley Church, and a monument in his memory was erected in Kensington Gardens, London.

## Robert Koch (1843–1910)

Robert Koch was born in Clausthal, Germany. His father was a mining official. Robert was very intelligent and taught himself to read at a very young age. He went to the local school, where he became interested in biology. In 1862 Koch went to the University of Gottingen to study medicine. After qualifying, he worked at hospitals in several cities in Germany. In 1866 he married Emmy Fraats, and they had one daughter, Gertrud. Koch traveled to Africa, Italy, India, England, and other countries for his work. He became famous and received awards and much praise. He was awarded the Nobel Prize for Physiology or Medicine in 1905. Koch died in 1910, in Baden-Baden, Germany.

## Joseph Lister (1827–1912)

Joseph Lister was born in Upton, Essex, England. His father was a wine merchant and scientist. The family were Quakers, and Joseph was sent to a Quaker school. He was interested in science and decided he wanted to be a doctor. He took an arts course in London, and then enrolled as a medical student in 1848. He worked at hospitals in London, Edinburgh, and Glasgow. Lister married Agnes Syme, the daughter of another surgeon, in 1856. Although they had no children, their marriage was happy. Lister was a shy man, more interested in his surgery and science than in money or honors. He was made a baronet in 1883. Agnes, his wife, died in 1892. The following year, Lister retired. In his last years, he was almost completely blind and deaf. Lister died in 1912 at Walmer in Kent, England.

## Louis Pasteur (1822–1895)

Louis Pasteur was born in Dole, France. At school Louis was good at art, but was not interested in science. He went to college in Paris, France and carried out research in physics, chemistry, and biology. In 1849 he married Marie Laurent, the daughter of a local priest. Although they had five children, only two survived. Pasteur spent his life teaching and carrying out research. In 1868 he became partly paralyzed and gave up teaching, but he carried on with his research. He was awarded honors by the French government, the Academie Française and several universities. Pasteur died in 1895 at Saint-Cloud, near Paris.

## Jonas Salk (1914–1995)

Jonas Salk was born in 1914 in New York. His family were poor, Russian-Jewish immigrants. He was the oldest of three boys. He was not interested in science at school and wanted to become a lawyer. His mother dissuaded him and instead he studied medicine in New York. He married Donna Lindsay in 1939, the same year as he qualified as a doctor. They had three children. After working for many years as a doctor, Salk switched to carrying out research. His development of the polio vaccine made him famous, and he was awarded honors by many countries. In 1968 Salk and Donna divorced, and in 1970 Salk married Françoise Gilot. He died in La Jolla, California in 1995.

# Glossary

**AIDS (Acquired Immune Deficiency Syndrome)** condition in which a person has a number of symptoms caused by damage to their body's defense system

**allergy** reaction by the body to a substance. For example, hay fever is an allergy to pollen.

**anthrax** deadly infectious disease caused by anthrax bacteria

**antibiotic** medicine that can kill bacteria and other microbes (but not viruses)

**antiseptic** chemical that is used to kill bacteria

**antitoxin** part of the blood from an infected individual that can be used to cure the same illness in other individuals

**cell** basic unit that makes up all living things. A cell contains a central nucleus surrounded by a gel-like substance called the cytoplasm. The nucleus and cytoplasm are surrounded by a wall or membrane.

**contaminate** make something impure by mixing unwanted material with it

**culture** liquid containing nutrients in which microbes or other cells can be grown

**diagnose** identify an illness

**diphtheria** infectious disease affecting the throat and breathing, caused by a bacterium named *Corynebacterium diphtheriae*

**epidemiology** study of the way a disease spreads

**ferment** change chemically by the action of microbes, such as yeast, in such a way that sugar turns to alcohol. For instance, grapes are fermented to make wine.

**HIV (Human Immunodeficiency Virus)** microorganism that infects a person and eventually causes them to get AIDS

**hygiene** cleanliness

**immune system** body's defenses against infection and disease

**inoculation** providing protection against a disease by injecting dead or weakened microbes into the body

**lysozyme** chemical that causes bacteria to burst open and die

**microbe** living thing that is too small to be seen without a microscope

**molecule** group of atoms that are joined together

**pasteurization** process of killing microbes by heating

**patent** obtain the legal right (from a government office) to make a particular product

**penicillin** common antibiotic

**pneumonia** inflammation of the lungs caused by a pneumococcus bacterium

**polio** disease, caused by the poliomyelitis virus, that can result in paralysis

**prescribe** recommend a particular medicine to treat an illness

**protein** large, complex group of molecules. Proteins form part of many body structures.

**pulse** regular beating of the blood in the main blood vessels carrying blood from the heart, especially as felt at the wrist

**pus** liquid that oozes from an infected wound

**resistance** body's ability to fight a disease

**serum** liquid part of the blood

**sewage** waste carried in sewers, normally including human waste and sometimes also including chemical waste

**sleeping sickness** infectious disease caused by a microbe, *Trypanosoma cruzi*, and spread by mosquitoes

**smallpox** infectious disease caused by the variola virus

**sterile** free of microbes

**sterilize** kill any microbes present

**tonsillitis** inflammation of the tonsils in the mouth and throat, caused by bacteria

**tuberculosis (TB)** disease that usually affects the lungs, caused by a bacterium named *Mycobacterium tuberculosis*

**vaccinate** provide protection against a disease by introducing dead or weakened microbes into the body

**virus** disease-causing microbe that is many times smaller than a bacterium

# Further Resources

If you have enjoyed this book and want to find out more, you can look at the following books and websites.

## Books

Alpin, Elaine Marie. *Germ Hunter: A Story About Louis Pasteur.* Minneapolis: Lerner Publishing Company, 2004.

Ballard, Carol. *Body Focus: The Immune System.* Chicago: Heinemann Library, 2004.

Bédoyère, Guy de la. *Milestones in Modern Science: The Discovery of Penicillin.* Milwaukee: Gareth Stevens, 2005.

Bédoyère, Guy de la. *Milestones in Modern Science: The First Polio Vaccine.* Milwaukee: Gareth Stevens, 2005.

## Websites

**Pharmaceutical Research and Manufacturers of America**
**www.innovation.org**
A project of the Pharmaceutical Research and Manufacturers of America, a good website for older readers.

**Pfizer Fun Zone**
**www.pfizerfunzone.com**
You can explore activities and articles about scientists while learning about many science topics on this educational website hosted by the pharmaceutical company, Pfizer Inc.

# Index

# Index